Fun with Maths

Compiled by John Drinkwater
Illustrated by Mike Gordon

Ladybird Books

Counting to 10

Here are the numbers from 0 to 10.

0	1	2	3	4	5	6	7	8	9	10
zero	one	two	three	four	five	six	seven	eight	nine	ten

Look at this picture of Joe the Clown.

Write the answers to the questions in the boxes.

How many buttons? 4

How many stars on Joe's jacket? 9

How many yellow stripes on Joe's trousers? 3

How many gloves? 1

How many stripes altogether on Joe's trousers?

How many spots on Joe's bow tie?

Colour the balls green.

Colour Joe's hat red.

Adding on

Here are the numbers from 1 to 20.

1 2 3 4 5 6 7 8 9 10 11 12 13 14 15 16 17 18 19 20

If you start on 6 and count on 3, you get to 9.

So, 6 **add on** 3 is 9.

6 + 3 = 9

8 + 2 = ☐

Using the number line at the top of the page to help you, fill in the boxes to complete the sums. The first one has been done for you.

Start	6	add 2	8	+ 1	9		
Start	3	add 1	4	+ 6	10		
Start	5	add 2		+ four		add 3	14
Start	4	add 2	6	+ 3		add 5	
Start	2	add 8		+ 5		add 5	
Start	7	+ nine		+ zero		add 4	

Taking away

Here are 7 bananas. The monkey eats 3 bananas.

There are 4 bananas left.

Here are 6 fish. 3 fish swim away.

How many fish are left? ☐

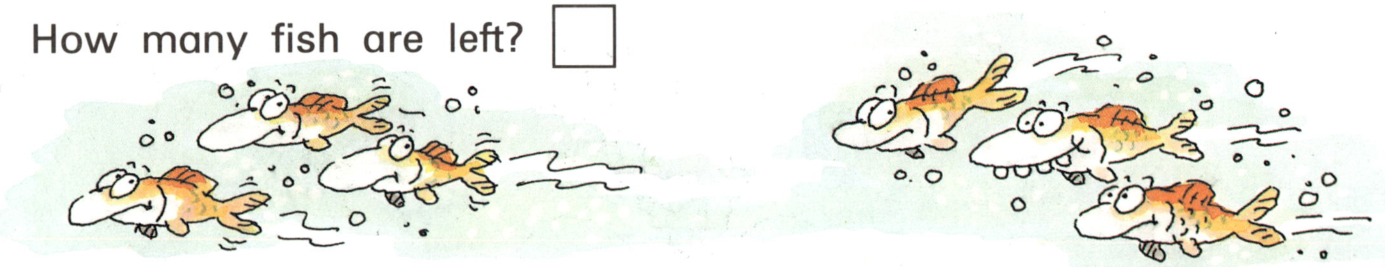

Here are 10 butterflies. 4 butterflies fly off.

How many butterflies are left? ☐

Here are 5 bones. The dog takes 1 bone away.

How many bones are left? ☐

Here are 12 birds. The cat chases 7 birds away.

How many birds are left? ☐

These are all words that we can use when we need to take one number away from another.

Five **take away** three equals two.

5 − 3 = 2

(5, 3) **difference** → 2 **subtract** 3 from 5 = 2 5 **minus** 3 = 2

Now try these. Write your answer in the box.

10 − 3 = ☐	(7, 4) difference ☐	11 minus 6 = ☐
9 − 3 = ☐	(8, 6) difference ☐	13 minus 7 = ☐
8 − 3 = ☐	(12, 7) difference ☐	15 minus 8 = ☐
7 − 3 = ☐	(17, 3) difference ☐	17 minus 9 = ☐
6 − 3 = ☐	(19, 12) difference ☐	19 minus 11 = ☐
5 − 3 = ☐	(20, 4) difference ☐	9 minus 3 = ☐

Answer ☐

Telling the time (1)

Some watches have two hands.
The longer hand shows the minutes.
The shorter hand shows the hours.

When the long hand points to 12 it says **o'clock.**

It is 4 o'clock.

What time do these clocks and watches show?

[8] o'clock [2] o'clock [11] o'clock [9] o'clock

Draw the long and short hands to show the time on these clocks.

6 o'clock 9 o'clock 11 o'clock 7 o'clock

Colour by numbers

Complete the sums to find out which colour to use.

Example: 22 + 3 = 25 = orange

number	25	17	9	31	4	15	10
colour	orange	yellow	red	green	brown	blue	purple

Tens and units

This group of trains has been put into sets of 10.

There are two sets of 10 and 3 single trains. | 2 | tens | 3 | units

Put these into sets of 10.

☐ tens ☐ units

20 tens 1 units

☐ tens ☐ units

Look at this number.

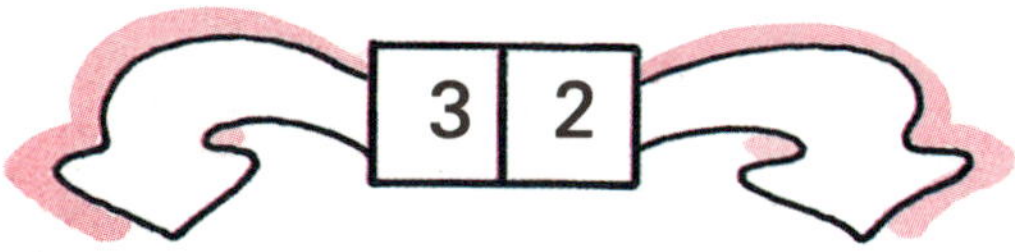

This tells you how many tens there are.

This tells you how many units there are.

Write down the tens and units in these numbers.

45
4 tens 5 units

22
☐ tens ☐ units

25
☐ tens ☐ units

13
☐ tens ☐ units

40
☐ tens ☐ units

39
☐ tens ☐ units

Now put the numbers in order, starting with the smallest.

13 → ☐ → ☐ → ☐ → ☐ → ☐

Telling the time (2)

When the long hand points to 6 it says **half past.**
What time do these clocks show?

__________ __________ __________ __________

Draw the long and short hands to show the time on these watches.

half past one

half past three

half past ten

When the long hand points to 3 it says **quarter past.**

It is quarter past four.

What time do these clocks show?

____________ ____________ ____________ ____________

When the long hand points to 9 it says **quarter to.**

It is quarter to six.

What time do these watches show?

____________ ____________ ____________ ____________

Draw the long and short hands to show the time on these watches.

quarter to one | quarter past eleven | quarter past two

Odds and evens

1	2	3	4	5	6	7	8	9	10
11	12	13	14	15	16	17	18	19	20

(blue) odd numbers
(red) even numbers

The snakes have swallowed some numbers. This snake has swallowed **even** numbers. Can you see which numbers they are? It will help if you trace over each number.

This snake has swallowed **odd** numbers.

Odd numbers always end with 1, 3, 5, 7 or 9.
Even numbers always end with 0, 2, 4, 6 or 8.

Join the dots to complete the picture.
You must join only the **odd** numbers.
Start at number 1.

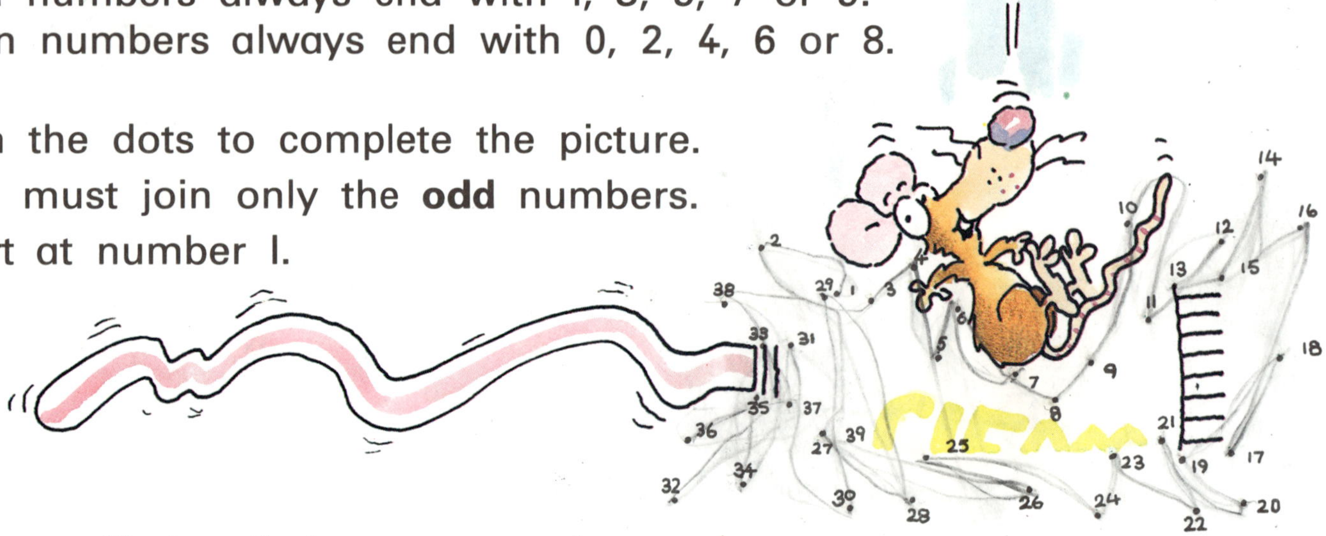

Circle all the **even** numbers.

33 16
6 41
16 66 23
ten
12 29
six one
11
12 nine

Favourite colours

I asked some of my friends what their favourite colours were. Here are their answers!

It's easy to draw a **block graph** to show which is the favourite colour. Three people liked red, so I can colour 3 blocks red.

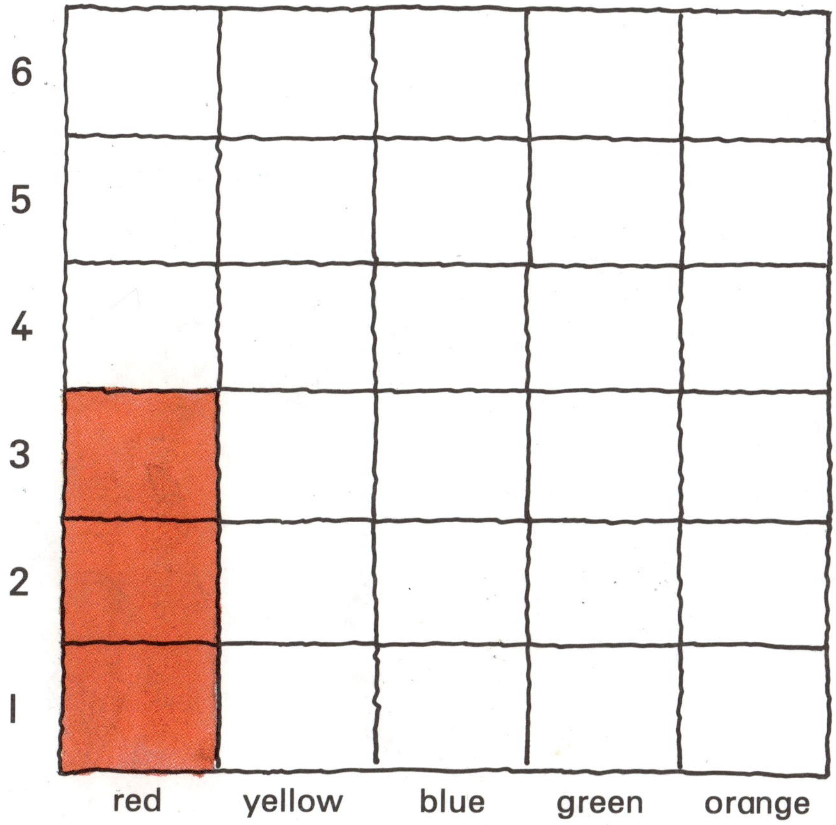

Complete the block graph by counting the favourite colours and filling in the blocks.

Which colour was the most popular? ___________

How many people took part in this survey? ☐

Repeated addition (multiplying)

Here are 3 cats. Each cat has 2 ears. How many ears are there altogether?

We can work this out by doing a long sum:

$2 + 2 + 2 = 6$

A quicker way of writing this would be to say there are

3 sets of 2 or $3\ (2) = 6$

If each cat has 4 legs, how many legs are there altogether?

$4 + 4 + 4 = \square$

$3\ (4) = \square$

When we do sums like this we usually write them as:

$3 \times 2 = 6$

$3 \times 4 = 12$

These are called **multiplication** sums.

Complete the following.

Here are 3 flowers. Each flower has 5 petals. How many petals altogether?

$\boxed{3} \times \boxed{5} = \square$

Here are 2 clowns. Each clown has 7 balloons. How many balloons altogether?

$\boxed{2} \times \square = \square$

Here are 2 cars. Each car has 4 wheels.
How many wheels altogether?

□ × □ = □

Here are 6 mice. Each has 1 tail, 2 eyes and 6 whiskers.

How many tails?

□ × □ = □

How many eyes?

□ × □ = □

How many whiskers?

□ × □ = □

Now try these.
You may like to use beads or counters to help you.

4 × 1 = □

2 × 2 = □

4 × 3 = □

6 × 2 = □

5 × 3 = □

7 × 2 = □

6 × 4 = □

4 × 5 = □

2 × 8 = □

There is a picture hidden in the box below. To find the picture, colour only the segments where the answer is 12.

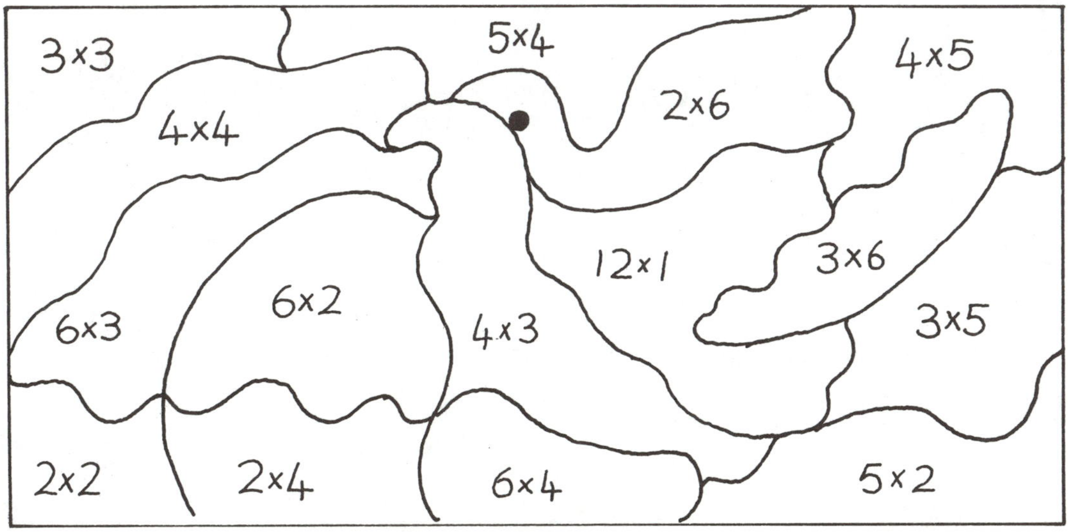

Sharing (dividing)

Here are 12 marbles.

If you had to share them equally among four friends, how many marbles would each friend get?

Try it with real marbles or other objects. Answer ☐

The marble problem can be turned into a sum.

12 shared among 4 can be written as $12 \div 4$

Each person gets 3 marbles so $12 \div 4 = 3$

This is called a **division** sum.

Share these sweets equally between two friends.

How many would each friend get?

$8 \div 2 =$ ☐

How many sweets would four friends get?

$8 \div 4 =$ ☐

Share these flowers equally between two vases.

How many flowers in each vase?

$16 \div 2 =$ ☐

Share these cherries equally among five cakes.

How many cherries on each cake?

20 ÷ 5 = ☐

Share these fish among seven bowls.

How many fish in each bowl?

14 ÷ 7 = ☐

Now try these sums. You may like to use real objects, such as marbles or buttons, to help you.

6 ÷ 3 = ☐	15 ÷ 5 = ☐	14 ÷ 2 = ☐
4 ÷ 2 = ☐	16 ÷ 8 = ☐	12 ÷ 6 = ☐
12 ÷ 3 = ☐	20 ÷ 4 = ☐	6 ÷ 2 = ☐
36 ÷ 6 = ☐	24 ÷ 4 = ☐	30 ÷ 5 = ☐

Symmetry

Look at these shapes. Each shape can be folded down the middle so that one half exactly matches the other half. We say that these shapes are **symmetrical**.

Try drawing these shapes yourself.
Cut them out and fold them in half.

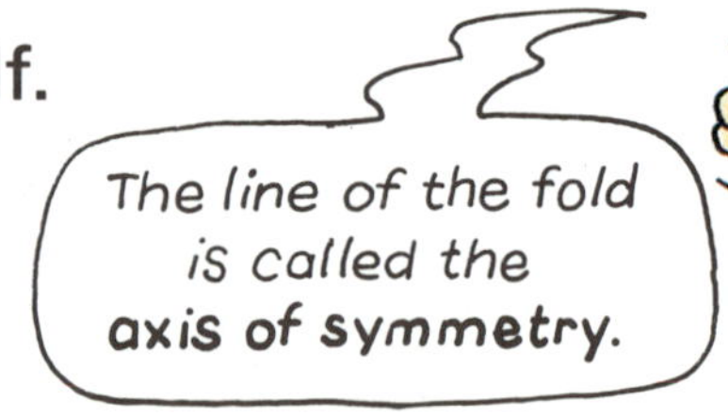

Draw in the **axis of symmetry** for these shapes.

Here the axis of symmetry has been drawn for you. Draw in the matching half of each picture.

Money

David has been sent to the shops to buy some fruit. Here are the coins he has been given.

How much money does David have altogether? ☐

How many apples can he buy? ☐

How much money would he have left? ☐

How many pears can he buy? ☐

How much money would he have left? ☐

How many oranges can he buy? ☐

How much money would he have left? ☐

David has one brother and one sister. How much money would he need to buy an apple, pear and orange each for himself and his brother and sister?

Answer ☐

Just five minutes more

The long hand of a watch is called the **minute hand.** It takes five minutes to move from one number to the next.

When the minute hand is moving between 12 and 6 it tells us how many minutes have passed since the hour began.

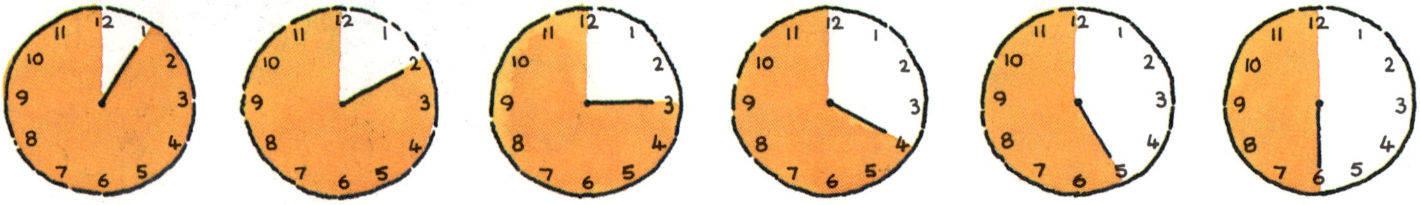

5 minutes past — 10 minutes past — 15 minutes (quarter) past — 20 minutes past — 25 minutes past — 30 minutes (half) past

This watch shows that 10 minutes have passed since it was 4 o'clock.

It is 10 minutes past 4.

Draw the hands on these clocks.

5 minutes past 3 — 25 minutes past 7 — 10 minutes past 9 — 20 minutes past 6

What time is shown on these watches?

__________ __________ __________ __________

When the minute hand is moving between 6 and 12 it tells us how many minutes there are before the next hour.

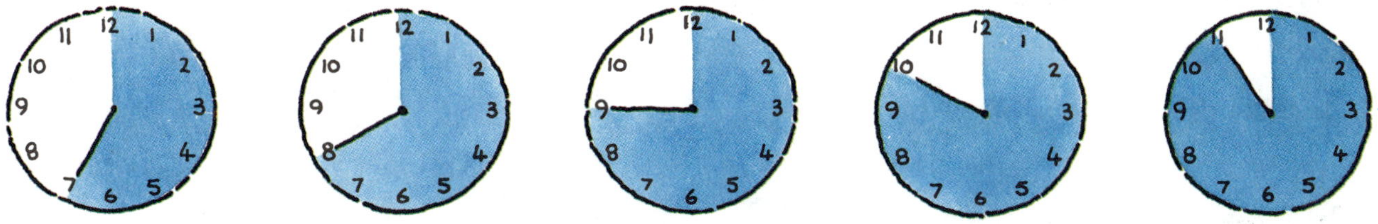

25 minutes to	20 minutes to	15 minutes (quarter) to	10 minutes to	5 minutes to

This watch shows it is 10 minutes before 7 o'clock.

It is 10 minutes to 7.

Draw the hands on these watches.

5 minutes to 5	20 minutes to 2	10 minutes to 4	25 minutes to 12	5 minutes to 8

What time is shown on these clocks?

An amazing maze

To work your way across the maze you must move from square to square either **sideways** or **downwards.**
You can only pass through squares where the answer to the sum is 24 or 10.

				Start					
3 × 4	6 ÷ 6	6 + 0	19 + 9	8 + 2	3 × 3	12 ÷ 2	6 + 6	7 × 3	15 ÷ 3
20 − 6	6 + 10	3 + 9	20 ÷ 5	6 × 4	20 ÷ 2	18 − 8	5 × 2	19 − 8	1 × 4
14 + 1	27 − 4	9 + 4	13 + 0	11 + 4	16 ÷ 8	4 × 4	8 × 3	10 + 0	9 + 8
17 + 2	8 + 8	8 × 2	3 + 12	17 − 2	28 ÷ 7	19 + 7	20 − 6	30 ÷ 3	7 + 11
14 − 7	12 × 1	1 × 4	4 ÷ 2	1 + 10	12 + 7	30 − 6	6 + 4	12 × 2	22 − 4
28 + 0	17 − 5	19 + 5	12 + 12	7 + 3	4 × 6	20 ÷ 2	12 − 5	1 + 8	30 − 3
24 ÷ 4	16 − 9	28 − 4	2 × 3	18 ÷ 2	8 + 3	6 × 0	15 ÷ 5	3 ÷ 3	21 + 6
6 × 1	5 + 7	2 × 5	10 − 0	28 − 4	14 ÷ 7	4 + 17	3 + 15	7 × 3	18 ÷ 9
				End					

Estimating to the nearest 10

Do not count the mice!
Estimate the number of mice.

Write your estimate here. ☐

Now count the mice. ☐

If there had been 38 we could say that there are **roughly 40 mice.**

If there had been 22 we could say that there are **roughly 20 mice.**

Roughly how many mice were there? ☐

Complete the following:

18 is roughly ☐

52 is roughly ☐

☐ is roughly 60

83 is roughly ☐

21 is roughly ☐

67 is roughly ☐

☐ is roughly 90

65 is roughly ☐

A twisty problem

You will need: scissors, 3 strips of paper 4 cm wide and 40 cm long (strips of newspaper will do), Sellotape.
(You may need a grown-up, too!)

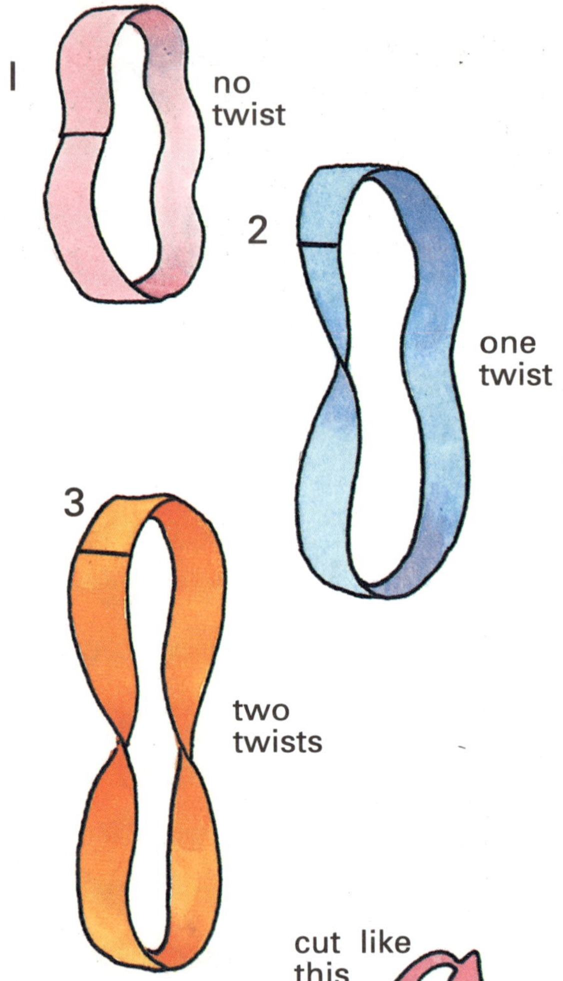

1 Join the ends of one strip of paper together to form a loop.

2 Join the ends of the second strip together to form a loop with one twist in it.

3 Join the ends of the third strip together to form a loop with two twists in it.

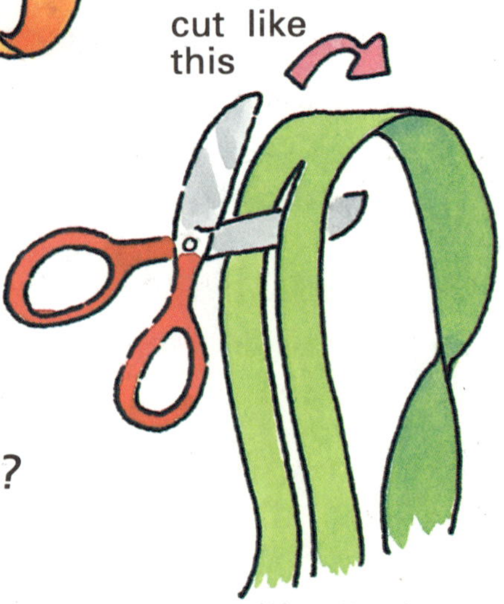

Cut each loop into two pieces starting with the first one that you made.
BUT before you start,
try to guess what
will happen when you
cut the loops.

Were you surprised by what happened?